Of Hungry Cats and Immortal Pigeons

Poems by
Farman Yusufzai

Order this book online at www.trafford.com
or email orders@trafford.com

Most Trafford titles are also available at major online book retailers.

First published in 1992 by Woodfield Publishers
Woodfield House, Arundel Road
Fontwell, Arundel, West Sussex. UK

Printed in Victoria, BC, Canada.

ISBN: 978-1-4269-2725-6 (sc)

*Our mission is to efficiently provide the world's finest, most comprehensive
book publishing service, enabling every author to experience success.
To find out how to publish your book, your way, and have it available
worldwide, visit us online at www.trafford.com*

Trafford rev. 9/8/2010

 www.trafford.com

North America & international
toll-free: 1 888 232 4444 (USA & Canada)
phone: 250 383 6864 ♦ fax: 812 355 4082

CONTENTS

· THE POEMS ·

· SECTION A · THE MONOCEROS

· SECTION B · THE PHOENIX

· SECTION C · THE CHAMELEON

· SECTION D · THE LUPUS

· SECTION E · THE AURIGA

· SECTION F · THE ARA

· SECTION G · THE PEGASUS

INTRODUCTION

"And isn't there virtue of verse that wasn't in the bard?"

I was first introduced to the work of Farman by a mutual friend. I was interested to read his poems, thinking he might benefit from my comments and suggestions. It was, of course, the patronising attitude of a typically ignorant Englishman. Once I had read his poetical work and his large collection of aphorisms, I quickly realised that here was a writer whose mastery of the English tongue was in need of no tutoring from me. On the contrary, I found that I needed to consult my dictionary in order to gain more fully from his use of vocabulary. The verse is written with such fluency and confidence that I was quickly able to settle down and enjoy the vistas and language which the poems present. Having defined myself above as a 'typically ignorant Englishman', I must confess that all I write here in this Introduction must be seen in that light. What I write here is my own view, my interpretation, of which the author was unsuspectingly ignorant. As I read the poems, I was deeply aware of Farman's broader, more inclusive perspective on life. I was aware of the multi-cultural appreciation of his mind, compared to the Englishness of my own. Themes of ancient India and Egypt, as well as the Judeo-Christian inheritance, all find echoes in the poems. More than ever, I was aware of the limitations of the education offered in the imperially dominated England since 1944. Images and inner-meanings must have passed me cleanly by, and for this I am duly saddened. My Introduction is, therefore, prefaced by an admission of inadequacy, not merely as a matter of form, or good manners, nor to excuse my omissions, but as a warning that the author of the poems is a much better read than the author of the Introduction.

Farman asked me to offer some philosophy of poetry as part of this introductory section. It was an impossible request. The impulse to write is indefinable, uncontrollable, and that is an essential part of its vitality. He himself addresses the issue in 'Sheshnag / in the basket of ribs' (p. 69). The poet begs to be inhabited and possessed by the creative forces of godhead. It seems that through unity with God, the author gains inspiration for his work. By accepting the closest possible liaison, the voice of inspiration is heard via the poet, a mere basket of ribs. The poet invokes godly inspiration and recognises the truth of his own phrase in 'shady games' (p. 19).

> 'And aren't there lips,
> warm with a smile
> that the artist didn't paint?
> and isn't there virtue of verse
> that wasn't in the bard?'

Such an invocation of God as true author and inspiration makes these poems religious verse. Throughout the collection, there is a pervading sense of God, and an express faith in some ultimate purposefulness. The poet sees humanity struggling against the deepest realities and trying to supplant them with transient issues and responses which deflect us from the truly satisfying experiences. The poems are gently persuasive testimonies to the reality of the deeper questions that life poses, but which we would prefer to neglect.

The poet presents a deterministic world picture against which he sees a humanity straining to resist. Reality demands acceptance, acquiescence, even submission. Only through acceptance of that which is most deeply true about life can humanity find peace and security. This acceptance leads to inner peace, but we feel as a continual distraction, what appears to be real fear, real hatred, real lust, and these cause us to strain against what would bring real happiness. In 'the wondering/wide-eyed lotus' (p. 72), we see a picture of a prince deeply set in meditation, losing himself and awareness of his physicality:

> 'The prince, sitting on a rush mat,
> shed no shadow,
> and let his inner light
> gild the temples of heaven'.

His 'grip on emptiness' is loosened by inner visions of his princess and they try to satisfy themselves, 'the wanting void of their souls' by their love.

The atmosphere of seductive charm is enhanced by the fragrance of the sandalwood trees, but the poem ends with:

'and the wide-eyed lotus in the pond nearby
wondered as never before'.

The lotus, the essence of dreamy forgetfulness and the loss of desire to return home, has worked its enchantment again. The prince's true home is not to be found through the distractions of arousal by a princess. This sounds like a theme which could be found in almost any religious tradition. But in this collection, the scenery and atmosphere is very definitely that of the Indo-Pakistan subcontinent. The author of this Introduction approaches the poems with the background of Western culture and finds himself sometimes bewildered by the sounds of Asia, but religion is one matter that can unite us, at a deep level. Religions are a way of dealing with experience. They are an attempt at describing reality. They offer a world-picture, a framework, in which the various parts of real life can be fitted, seen in relationship, and understood. In different ages and varying climates, they may look at odds with each other, propose clashing pantheons, and use strangely conflicting images. They all, in fact, draw on human experience, human situations, as their wellspring. So, all religions should be within the reach of a sympathetic person to understand. Often, what makes religion exciting is the way in which it addresses the disasters and pain of human experience. The world-picture is the backdrop against which the tragedy is explainable. No matter that some parts do not seem to fit into the picture. Paradoxically, paradoxes prove helpful! Absurdities are a spur to deeper assimilation into the whole picture. Religion helps us to cope with the shocking, the unimaginable, the searingly painful, by providing a notation in which the world may be heard as harmony, pleasing and satisfying in all its parts. Such dissonance as may be heard is merely the as yet unresolved aspect of the overriding harmonious structure. The overriding feeling in this collection is the conflict within the human condition by which we waste our energy and life trying to resolve and satisfy issues which are unimportant distractions from the real questions which we are unable to see because of our concentration on the more transient side of life. The poems depict with great sympathy, or is it empathy, an insight into human weakness, little foibles, pride, self seeking, selfishness, which speak of the inner emptiness of our lives. They are surrounded by a sense of impending doom which is recorded with full weight, but without panic, and in a resigned manner. The author is not above us, but speaks as one who knows what it means to be a weak human being.

Farman sees the world around him poetically and responds with an attempt to see life from all sides, to be prepared to look at 'the other side / of the picture' (p. 57). In the poem of that name, he describes his childhood innocent attempt to turn a picture round in order to see the other side:

> 'And even now that I'm older,
> and should know better,
> I cannot shut my eyes,
> even if my winkless gaze blinds me.
> I cannot, I cannot keep from looking
> for the other side
> of the picture'.

This simple image is a key to so much that is in the searching spirit of Farman. He is unwilling to accept how things appear to be without the deepest enquiry and scrutiny. He rejects the mono-cultural solution which is subject to 'this crippling hold/of 'one" (p. 14). In so doing, he ranges freely across the cultural parameters in a manner that avoids syncretism by virtue of its strongly individual motivation and its very personal voice. We feel that we are in a recognisable scene, say a scented evening in a distant Asian clime, and then the Book of Genesis suddenly emerges from the page. Such is the case in 'in dusk/ at eventide' (p. 44). A prophet has been giving the world the benefit of his wisdom, and as evening dusk descends, he starts his journey home, obviously well-content with his own contribution, his concepts and descriptions. Then, he sees a snake in his path and he is triggered back to his primeval fears.

> "Snake', hissed the very seed of man in him.
> Only moments ago, fearless and firm,
> he had uttered the word that had within it
> the beginning, the middle and the end

of everything that he knew
and everything he didn't
and now the utterer of the last word
on the fate of the world
stood frozen with terror'.

He has in fact, in the dusk, mistaken a ragged piece of rope for a snake, but he is reduced from his independent, self-important public image to a more natural, more attractive, more down-to-earth person:

'He stood frozen with terror,
until his feet, knowing better,
led him back to the doorstep
where mate and child waited,
in dusk
at eventide'.

It is the feet, the point of contact with solid earth, which lead him away from both his high-flown theories and his primitive terrors. They lead him back to the fulcrum of expression for human life, the familial scene, the love of mate and child. For the poet, left outside the influence of male fantasy, women are by far more noble and natural and good. Concerned, as they are, with the reality of human contact, they are saved from the precarious flights of unearthed male imaginations. The themes of lack-of-earth-contact and high-flown masculine fantasy find expression in the poems which try and draw primeval themes together with such modern ideas as space flight.

The themes are intermingled with the poet's sense of the permanent round of procreation on which humans set so much store, but which seems to get nowhere, except to deliver yet another generation which then struggles with the same interminable human dilemmas. In 'make believe/of make-believe' (p. 48), there is an apocalyptic vision in which the cycle of life from apes to men is swiftly described as 'some players' who stage a make-believe, in which apes ape men, and men look on in alien disgust.

'And while men looked on,
the homesick apes,

riding mutant freaks,
travelled all the way, from the launching site,
to the forest of their forefathers,
and back –
only to find the audience
gone'.

In 'the good news is/they're breeding apace' (p. 41), the poet links aeons by bringing together 'the seed that sprouted' in the 'depths of the slime' and a couple who 'built a flying cave', in which they left earth to colonise the stars. Thus linked, primeval life forms groping for successful emergence in the natural selection of species are shown to be fundamentally at one with the superficially superior creator of technology whose creative genius takes him potentially toward galactic travel, but who is still grunting away at procreation. Whether in the slime or in the throes of space exploration, the same realities both confront and elude our race, with its self-importance and its refusal to undertake the all important journey of inner-space travel. The same effect is created in 'a house of cards' (p. 11), in which

'anything and everything
from lunar visits,
and genetic engineering,
to galactic travel,
and the all-bionic human,
is achievable'.

But none of this prevents man's creation being still a house of cards. In 'the countdown/to zero' (p. 9), the natural world and space jargon are bonded with better effect. The poem is a graphic account of the determinism present in the collection as a whole. The descent of a leaf from a tree, moved on the crest of a breeze, is described as 'along a mapped out path'. The leaf lands on top of a wood-louse. The fall of the leaf has attracted the attention of a curious chick who eyes it as it descends to earth.

'and as the countdown got to zero
the chick's beak struck.

One well-aimed peck
pierced the leaf and the wood-louse,
and the wood-louse ended up
in the chick's hungry gizzard
as indifferent food'.

The everyday tale is described using the terminology of a tense countdown at a space-centre, but the very basic, even uninteresting event they count down towards is so lacking in notability. And herein lies the irony. Our scientific powers are wasted on pursuits which have similarly little or no satisfaction for us. Our human potential is dissipated and wasted. And again, the irony is redoubled as we learn that our misuse of our brains may well end in our race being pecked off the face of the earth without us ever knowing how or when it was going to happen. Our ultimate fate may be as totally inconceivable to us as the life of a spacecraft is to a wood-louse or even a chick.

So the poet profoundly questions human striving and human determination to make the world work for us like a machine. He suggests that there is a state of beyond-knowing, freed from the self-importance of knowing and the painful search for knowing. In 'song/of never know' (p. 73), he describes the state in enchanting terms. He contradicts the 'I know' as being the burden of the song of 'never know' which fills the shell of the world. In a melodic stanza, he writes:

'Round and round the singers go
around the centre of never know
while the grove is all gold,
with basant and its maids,
who sing the truth
of bhakti and love,
which they seem to know
rather well'.

He then describes a state, blessed it would seem, in which all the contradictions of knowing or not knowing are resolved:

'until knowing
and not knowing

and seeming to know are the same
and the grove, all gold,
with basant and its maids,
is everywhere'.

The images look appealing, even seductive, and I wonder if they are also arousing, in a way which distracts from the inner search?

As a westerner, the impression I have gained from a general education about Asian religions is one in which the individual person is seen as part of the creative cycle of life, renewed and renewing in turn, and in which a person may find deep affinity with the more striking examples of life around. In 'the sunbright soul' (p. 70), there is a powerful evocation of the cobra, a snake as magnificent and majestic as it is deadly.

The poet urges his heart to merge with the heart of the cobra. He describes the cobra's neck as:

'crowned with a head
carved out of benumbing terror,
bejewelled with bedevilling eyes
that no veil, no darkness know'.

The stunned admiration for the cobra's visual power and deadly potency are well communicated. One has an inner vision of the cobra's head even brighter than the bright Indian sun behind it, and at the centre of the whole picture, a soul of 'glistening black glory'.

'And when the cobra's head,
and you, my heart, are one,
the glistening black glory
of the sunbright soul of the cobra
will be mine too'.

The Eastern religious scene is expressed again with power in 'in Banaras' (p. 71). Reincarnation of the soul of all life is a gradual movement towards a fulfilling reunification with the origin of life. Human memory is able, at times, to recapture some of the discarded shades of lives:

'The tentacles of my memory
are recoiling
along the existence-extinction continuum'.

The poet remembers the past as the 'symbiotic cohabitation' of life and death and describes it as 'wanton pleasure'. And yet, he now seems to have lost something of the rhythm of that faith insight. The present seems ever too present. He wishes to recoil, to recapture the progress towards ultimate satisfaction. He remembers a time:

'Ah, that was the time
when life and death
danced and danced and danced,
like the anklet-laden feet
of a temple dancer dancing to Shiva,
her gazelle eyes wondering and worshipping
and the curves of her redolent presence
melting in music,
in a temple in Banaras'.

Perhaps the poet is here sighing for the loss of faith? Perhaps he is now describing his abandonment of the basic concept of the faith, this reincarnation, and now, he longs for the possibility that it was still true, that he could still believe it? Or perhaps he is accepting the reality of his own human weakness, a weakness that will launch him into an infinity of searching and wandering.

'Such are the tics
our protoplasmic clay is corrupt with,
and will, for ever, be slave to an infinity
of dislodged, disowned, desolate ghosts'.

The pathos is poignant, the human sense of inadequacy universal, the persona of the poet archetypal. This same quality is also found in 'the laggard bidder' (p. 58), where there is a painful image of a bidder at an auction whose 'befogged, befuddled' wits can never quite propel him to make a bid which will end his permanent attendance in the auctioneer's sale room. He is held up by the conventional question about the meaning of it all:

> "Why, why indeed?'
> and a shade more lost than before,
> back to his corner he went,
> and slept,
> until the doors opened again'.

In 'worm's lament' (p. 55), the poet creates a striking metaphor of the human condition. The worm addresses a man, whose foot has caused mayhem with the world of worms, wrecking homes and causing panic. Man seems a mighty monster to worm. Man swerves his foot to avoid crushing worm, but worm unimpressed by the godlike Man, uses the event not to express gratitude, but to pinpoint its sense of grievance with the dispensation emanating from the mighty Man. The worm speaks for humanity set against the dispensations of our mighty deities. The worm asks:

> 'You wrecked our homes,
> why, then, did you spare
> this wormy, slimy life of mine?'

It is a pertinent question for many people in all ages. What is the value of living 'under the Himalayan weight of life?'. The worm calls into question the inner sincerity of the man's swerving foot.

> 'O god of gods, did you hope
> to prove to yourself thus
> the quality of your spirit?'

The worm asks if Man would have reacted differently had it been a case of his brother:

> 'the magnificent serpent –
> the one that performed better
> than you and your god?'

Always on the look out for the weak point of man, the worm assumes false humility, or hurt feelings:

> 'Tell me if you would have me vanish
> into the rare comfort of my blind burrow.
> Or, shall I, like a good little gadget,
> go on tilling your earth, O King?'

Worm now returns to questioning the motives of Man's avoidance of a deadly footfall. Was it a lack of curiosity, he goads Man, or was it just an urge to extend the misery of life? Or was there something inherent in the anatomy of the foot that shrank away from the terror of crushing? The jaunty, terrified, philosophising worm is a caricature, but he looks very familiar. He is a demanding, ungrateful, unsatisfied, two-dimensional creature, and quite unable to comprehend the subtleties and possibilities of the man's nature. Human limitations are seen in the same light, and beyond our world, there is a hint of even greater worlds and ever more incomprehensible layers of relationship and meaning. The poem works well and provokes a thoughtful response. The poet succeeds in a searching portrayal of the origins of evil in 'Jinni' (p. 74). He sets out a mythology of a mighty 'I', who grew in fiendish ways until at last it became possible to engender a personified evil, Jinni.

> 'I willed with all my might
> and my womb threw up Jinni,
> the mightiest of monsters'.

The infant Jinni is taught all the tricks of the evil trade:

> 'to coo, to hiss,
> to growl, to howl,
> the winsome smile, the fearsome frown'.

Jinni is allowed to roam around the universe destroying at will. But eventually, Jinni dies completely and cries to be subsumed in 'I' again.

'Save me, my source and sustenance,
in you alone I can exist,
for you alone are the void,
that is vacuous enough to hold me'

The urge to destruction and violence is seen as residing in the selfishness, the absolute selfishness of humanity. Self-will not only destroys others but it is also the cardinal sin that prevents progress and deepest joy. In this dramatic image, the poet suggests the power of self-generated evil, but also hints, at the close, of some assuaging, some ageing, which will bring relief and, hopefully, no repetition of the urge to destroy. This human tendency to tyranny makes him an outcast, puts him in a category apart from other creatures. But the time for a fresh start can come, perhaps, and may be taken, when it presents itself. In 'shed horns/cast skin/moult' (p. 2), the poet senses a time when the human race may achieve acceptance again But first it will have:

'to shed horns,
cast skin,
moult,
and begin all over again'.

Then, and only then, the rest of creation might again welcome us back into the fold. The poem is a touching evocation of human guilt tinged with real regret, or repentance. It has the marks of the recidivist who longs for normal life again after years of soul-destroying wickedness, or life-wasting addiction. The poem communicates a sense of longing for lost innocence and forgotten purposes. Humanity yearns to be what it was made to be, discover the peace it was created to enjoy, take its place in the created order that it was designed to fulfil. It desires the moment, the hour, when this will all become possible. In the meantime, it may be necessary to seek 'shelter/any shelter' (p. 54). In the poem of that name, Farman recounts his experience of finding a fish 'cosily lodged/in the carcass of another', in his fishbowl. His immediate reaction is outrage at the seeming act of cannibalism, a soulless, disgusting activity. But on reflection, he sees the other side of the picture, and finds sympathy with the fish's dilemma.

> 'Or was it just another bit of life,
> that had managed to find shelter –
> any shelter?'

This rapport with another creature, even one as remote from human activity as a fish in a fishbowl, speaks volumes for the sensitivity of the author as both a man and a poet. His work describes emotions and situations which have a universal basis and a cross-cultural application, though he uses predominantly the imagery and atmosphere of the East to achieve the end. The language and syntax, the images and the world-picture, the arousal of emotions of disgust or desire, and the wistful, yearning quality so central to the whole collection, all combine in an exciting and polished result.

I have quoted from several of Farman's poems in this Introduction but I could quite easily have quoted from them all. His work has an even quality. It is easy and attractive to read. It is warmly provocative and dwells on the deepest human themes of power, death, fear, sex, guilt, and love and the desire for unity and ultimate satisfaction. These poems will leave a lasting impression on the reader and, I hope, encourage the poet to publish more, and write more from the obviously wide experiences of his life and the deep reflection through which he has clearly put this experience.

I said at the beginning that these poems were 'religious' and so they are in that they are testimonies to the true struggle of humanity to understand the worst of human life, and cope with that, at the same time as believing in a purer, wholesome humanity. Farman's own personality shines through, as that of a good man, a balanced and mature observer, a patient listener, a reconciling spirit, in many ways, a voice out of our time. I hope that the accurate portrayal, but loving affirmation of humanity in these poems will be heard by all who read them, and that they will take their message of possibilities into a wider arena. This typically ignorant Englishman was moved by the experience of reading these poems, and his interest in the ways of the East were aroused considerably. He hopes his ignorance neither undersells the poetry nor offends the poet, and he offers this Introduction as an expression of his admiration.

Neil Richardson
The Rectory, Greenford Magna, 1992

PREFACE BY THE POET

I started writing English poetry in 1959. Some of the poems were published in magazines and anthologies in Pakistan and India. As a matter of fact it was my English poetry that landed me in Britain six years later. This is how it came about.

Way back in 1964 I decided to have someone of consequence comment on my poems. Bertrand Russell seemed to be a reasonable choice. I sent him some of my poems. He wrote back commenting that the poems were 'admirable' and that 'they represent the despairing bewilderment of our age'. This encouraged me to take my poetic sensibility a little more seriously.

A year later I read out my poem 'worm/to man', now entitled 'worm's lament', at an English poetry symposium, organised by the Karachi Arts Council. The symposium was presided over by Dr. H.R. Dodd, English Language Officer of the British Council at that time. After the symposium Dr. Dodd said to me,

'You must visit the mother country.'

'Britain?' I asked.

"Yes,' he said, 'Talking of English, Britain *is* the mother country, you would agree,' he explained.

Prompted thus, I came over to Britain and continued writing poetry.

* * *

What I have said in these poems, and the way I have said it, has been a source of much satisfaction to me. The reason, I think, is my belief that it would be a pity if a person appeared on the stage of the world, stayed on it for more or less three quarters of a century, and left it without recording his or her view of life in some form. These poems have saved me from that tragedy.

Once I was asked the unanswerable question as to how these poems came to be written in this particular style. The only answer I managed to give was that, as a baby finds joy in the arms of its own very special mother, as the ocean current finds its own course, as the birds in migration find the right direction to fly in, so did these poems find their own style. My poetic sensibility, I think, could not wear another garb.

As a foetus needs a womb to be formed in, the idea needs a style, with the difference that while the foetus cannot create a womb, the idea can create the style it needs. My poetry has done just that.

All poetry attempts to bridge the gulf between the word and the referent. So does mine. But, sadly, to attempt this is to attempt the impossible, I confess to have attempted the impossible. The results are before you. True, that 'all that's spoke is marr'd', as Gratiano bewailed, but I hope that in these poems the words used have not marred the idea, that the elemental nature of the idea has saved it from distortion.

It has been remarked that these poems are best read aloud. I leave it to the reader to judge if the remark is correct.

If something like a message or a moral emerges from a part of the collection or the collection as a whole, I assure the reader that I have not meant it.

Finally, I must confess I am exposing myself to the charge of presumptuousness but I will be dishonest to myself if I left unexpressed my belief that the form and style of these poems – particularly of the five poems of section G. *The Pegasus*, is going to be adopted, consciously or unconsciously, by many poets.

Farman Yusufzai

ACKNOWLEDGEMENTS

First I must acknowledge the debt I owe to Bertrand Russell, which is apparent from the episode I have described in the beginning of the Preface. It was his interest in my poems which proved to be an unfading impetus for me to continue writing poetry.

The perceptive comments and helpful suggestions made by my friends Carl Munn, Steve Earl and Aileen Dekker, have been helpful in enabling me to make several improvements in the manuscript. I thank them heartily.

I am grateful to my friend Hari Joshi for adding to my understanding of the religious and mythological concepts of Hinduism, which the reader will come across in Section H, *The Serpens*.

Dr. R.S. McGregor of the University of Cambridge, Dr. D. Matthews of the University of London, Dr. Sarah Mills and Mr. Peter Lewis of Loughborough University and Mr. James Pailing of Keble College, the University of Oxford read the poems and helped with useful comments. I thank them.

Fellow poet Neil Richardson not only wrote the introduction to the collection but also helped with looking at the poems critically. His valuable suggestions led to many significant changes in the manuscript. Furthermore, if he had not kept asking me for a firm date of completion of the manuscript, it would still be lying unfinished. My gratitude to him is beyond words.

I thankfully acknowledge the permission of Transworld Publishers Limited for the use of certain meanings from Stephen Hawking's book, *A Brief History of Time from the Big Bang to Black Holes'*. The meanings, followed by 'B.H.T. – Hawking' appear in '*Notes on Expressions in the Text Followed by Numbers'*. The permission has been granted via their copyright line, © Space Time Publications 1988.

Names of other books too, which I acknowledge as sources of meanings of some other expressions used in the collection, are given, along with the names of their publishers, in the said 'Notes'.

And, finally, I must acknowledge my indebtedness to my wife, Noor, and my daughter, Shameela, for the benefit I derived from the discussions I had with them regarding the finer shades of meanings of certain expressions. And let my confession be on record that their searching remarks about both the content and form of the poems have been so incisive and penetrating that sometimes I thought they understood what I meant better than I did.

A WORD ABOUT THE GROUPING OF THE POEMS INTO SECTIONS

Like stellar clusters in the night sky, the sixty-five poems fall into ten groups according to the ten different worlds of thought and feeling to which the poems in each group belong. Thus each of the ten groups, or "sections", as I have called them, reflects a closer unity of vision than the unity of the poetic vision of the collection as a whole. This reminded me of the names of the constellations of the Northern and Southern hemispheres and I realised that ten of them conjured up before the mind's eye the visions which suffuse the ten sections. I have, therefore, used them as titles of the sections.

For notes on these names please refer to the contents.

· THE POEMS ·

· Section A ·
The Monoceros

my first
and last love

Like an aborted foetus,
I'm more dead than dead.

But life being my first
and last love.
I must seek it out again,
sometime,
somewhere,
even if I have to travel
beyond the red shift[1],
to the birthplace of stars.

In the meantime, though,
what's driving me mad is the worry
that my resurrected self
might not be me.

shed horns
cast skin
moult

The water-demon
is big with life again,
and the lily on quiet waters
is wet with blood.

The time is ripe
to shed horns,
cast skin,
moult,
and begin all over again.

And who knows,
the beast, the bird and the reptile
might even want me back
in the fold.

transplants

There are three kinds of transplant:
the homotransplant[2],
the heterotransplant[3],
and the autotransplant[4].

Tom they saved with a homotransplant,
Dick with a heterotransplant,
and Harry with an autotransplant.

Now, let's not go into the why
and the wherefore of it all.
Let's just celebrate.
Long live Tom!
Long live Dick!
Long live Harry!

And if you ask,
what's the good
of a second chance to live?
I'll ask,
what's the good of the first?
Nonetheless, let us all rejoice
that Tom, Dick and Harry,
are still alive and kicking.

themselves again

They drive beast out of man
to make man better than man.

They drive man out of god
to make god better than god.

But do what they will,
the beast works its way
back into man,
and man works his way
back into god.

And thus, for the good of all,
beast and man and god
become themselves again.

**and then we will sleep
like newborns**

Come, the disowned and the deprived
of the world of my body,
and the world of my mind,
open your heart to me,
and I will open mine to you.
Tell me your tale,
and I will tell you mine.
Let us chant to the rumble of the future,
and to the echoes of the past.
Let us sing the song of coming together,
and the song of fruitfulness.

And then,
nestled against each other,
we will sleep
like newborns.

advantage

Now that your pet is dead,
it's a better pet.
Get it stuffed,
and you'll have your pet back,
with the added advantage,
that now you won't have
to collar it,
to feed it,
to walk it,
and to see it die.

· Section B ·
The Phoenix

the countdown
to zero

The countdown began
when a ripple of breeze moved
towards a chosen autumn leaf
that hung from a chosen branch
of a chosen tree.

It hit the target.
The leaf broke off,
and its earthbound journey began
along a mapped out path.

Finally, the leaf landed
on a particular wood-louse,
that had stopped for a fateful moment
on top of a marked out lump of soil
below the chosen tree.

Now, the eyes of a curious chick
had followed the leaf all along,
and as the countdown got to zero,
the chick's beak struck.
One, well-aimed peck
pierced the leaf and the wood-louse,
and the wood-louse ended up
in the chick's hungry gizzard
as indifferent food.

building nothing
out of nothing

While I owned the world,
all that I did
was to plunder it,
and finally,
I reduced it to rubble.

And now all that is left
of the world
and me, its erstwhile owner,
is a cosmic cemetery,
and its ghostly keeper.

But I will rise again and again,
and to match eternal folly
with eternal futility,
I will go on building
nothing,
out of nothing.

a house of cards

It is all a house of cards.
Man has built so much,
and so well
on the foundation of numbers –
the master mental constructs.

The spectacle
of this house of cards
is more than magnificent.
It is sublime.

In this house of cards, it seems,
anything and everything,
from lunar visits,
and genetic engineering,
to galactic travel,
and the all-bionic human,
is achievable.

But does all this
prevent this house of cards
from being what it is –
a house of cards?

whereabouts

The mathematician theorised,
and gave to the seeker
the whereabouts of truth.
'You'll find truth', he declared,
somewhere.....somewhere.....
between probability and improbability,
between certainty and uncertainty'.

Poor seeker of truth!
He looked for truth
all along the probability-improbability curve,
all along the certainty-uncertainty axis,
until he collapsed
in the midst of the maze
of a's which aren't a's
and b's which aren't b's
and the maze devoured him,
as the hungry whirlpool swallowed the straw,
as the thirsty desert sucked the raindrop in.

**what if the deities die
and the digits lie?**

For dear life
we thought up deities,
and we thought up digits.

And so far,
our deities in Heaven,
and in Hades[5],
and our digits,
as high above the cipher,
as below it,
have worked well.

But what if the deities die,
and the digits lie?

this crippling hold
of 'one'

What is so special about 'one'?
Why let it twist all thinking,
thwart all search?

One source, one beginning, one essence
of all that was, is, and shall be
is a fantasy of simple minds.

Can one seed grow into all the trees?
Can one tree bear all the fruits?

Couldn't the locksmith,
trying to cut one key
to all the locks,
use his skill to a better end?

Will the traveller,
trying to discover one route
to everywhere
ever get anywhere?

It's time
the human mind freed itself
of this crippling hold
of 'one'.

the lab dog

In the laboratory
he got an extra head.
Adrift in space, the two heads,
equipped with their own
individual pairs of eyes,
looked in different directions,
and barked out of key,
filling with noise
their brave new world,--
a lone, infecund void.

That's the kind of exercise,
that could do a lot of good
to us, humans.
Think.
Wouldn't life be
very much more like life,
if each of us
had several extra heads,
each head fitted with its own
individual pair of eyes,
each pair looking
in a different direction,
trying to find its truth
in its own way?

· *Section C* ·
The Chameleon

shady games

A mechanical friend of mine—
a perfect tamer of matter,
the other day complained
of an engine of his making
that wouldn't stop.

Out of the hands of a potter
fell his masterpiece,
and was dust –
dust that would never be
his masterpiece again.

And aren't there lips
warm with a smile,
that the artist didn't paint?
and isn't there virtue of verse
that wasn't in the bard?

What is going on?
Well, the master puppeteer must know.
and he might even tell me,
for we have been mates from the time
when we used to play shady games
in an alley
blind at both ends.

the good, old welder †

The good, old welder is a maker.
At his touch things come together,
not fall apart.

From the right
came the Justice of the Peace,
and amiably said,
"Welder, my good man, could you weld
the broken grip of my walking stick?"
"Gladly, Sir," said the welder,
and welded the grip.

A killer came from the left,
and growled,
"Welder, old man,
weld the broken grip of my dagger,
or else you die."

The welder smiled,
and quietly welded the grip.

With the dagger,
the killer has gone
on the kill once more.
Stick in hand,
the Justice of the Peace
is plodding along to his court again.

† The dagger and the walking stick which bracket the page numbers represent the ones which the killer
and the Justice of the Peace took to 'the good old welder'.

sleep,
or better still, die

Time is unconquerable.
All power buckles
before the might of Time,
we are told.

And yet, to conquer Time,
all that you have to do
is to sleep,
or better still,
die.

For sleep benights its vision,
and death strikes it dead.

the trapdoor clicks †

Click, click, the trapdoor clicks.
Click, it opens; click, it shuts.
Now it's life, now it's death,
now it's doing, now undoing,
on hinges of time, in depths of space,
on astral face, in womb and tomb.
Click, click, the trapdoor clicks.
Click, it opens; click, it shuts.

Click, click, the trapdoor clicks.
Click, it opens; click, it shuts.
Now it's come, now it's go,
now it's pull, now it's push,
with rational trick, with witless tact,
with open wings, with lopped off limbs.
Click, click, the trapdoor clicks.
Click, it opens; click, it shuts.

Click, click, the trapdoor clicks.
Click, it opens, click, it shuts.
Now it's chance, now mischance,
now it's adding, nothing and nothing,
now subtracting all from all,
getting all and nought mixed up.
Click, click, the trapdoor clicks.
Click, it opens; click, it shuts.

† Written to be acted out and sung at a college concert.

22

Click, click, the trapdoor clicks.
Click, it opens; click, it shuts.
Now it's sink, now it's swim,
now it's making, now unmaking,
for value, for wisdom, for death, for decay,
in the name of right, for the right of wrong.
Click, click, the trapdoor clicks.
Click, it opens, click, it shuts.

Click, click, the trapdoor clicks.
Click, it opens; click, it shuts,
with robot reach, with laser eye,
with faith in future, as a matter of faith.
It's hide and seek, it's touch and go,
it's fact, it's farce, of this and that.
Click, click, the trapdoor clicks.
Click, it opens; click it shuts.

the underground

If you are at Baker Street.†
Stanmore†, your destination,
isn't too far.
But it is, if you've drifted
to Oxford Circus†,
and believe it or not,
now you're heading
for the Elephant and Castle†,
not Stanmore†, by any means.
Go back, then, to the beginning,
to Baker Street†, that is,
and thank your stars,
that the going back isn't
all the way from the end,
from the Elephant and Castle†, that is.

However, it wouldn't really matter
whether you went
back to the beginning,
or forward to the end,
for the moment you board
an underground train,
you've total freedom
of inner space.

†London Underground stations

truth serum

As the heart can be made
to squirt out blood
with a dagger thrust,
so can the tongue be made
to blurt out truth
by injecting one's blood
with the truth serum.

There's a difference, though.
While the blood comes from the heart,
which has it,
truth comes from the tongue,
which has it not.

Where is the truth, then?
Where else, indeed,
if not in the truth serum itself?
Truth lies firmly lodged
between its molecules
and can be had in the free state
by treating the serum
with a well tortured man,
for, it is great pain alone
that can force truth out
of its honeycomb home
in the truth serum.

rapprochement

Let us thank our stars, things,
that, at least, one of us talks,
and is not cold and dumb.

And talk as I must,
I will tell you a thing or two.
Things, you are frigid.
Warm up to me, things.
I say strip, split.
Let me see your frozen heart
beat again.
Come, take me.
Sink your claws into my soft sides,
and haul me whole
deep into you,
for, if you don't,
we will, severally, wither away.

Listen, things.
We have fallen out for no good reason.
Don't you see, whatever we are,
we are, because of each other?

Let us cease to be aliens
to each other.
Be mine, things,
and I will be yours.

· *Section D* ·
The Lupus

**beware
of the wiles of life**

Beware of the wiles of life.
Reject the dreams and delusions
it confounds you with.
Deny its suspect ends
and shifty means,
and when it threatens doom,
laugh.

Yes, laugh away the idle threat,
and then it will know
that you know,
and will stand unclad
before your seeing eyes,
to win you over
with generous abandon
and the promise
of total fulfillment.

night after night, after night

Night after night, after night,
he and she,
work their bodies to full potential,
for pleasure, they think.

Their pleasure?
Or that of the god
of vermin?

when you kiss me

When you kiss me,
you kiss the mouth
of a born liar,
and also the mouth
that made the word
of the maker.

I am the source and the seat
of hordes of gods,
and of slayers of them all.
I hold within me
the prophet and the poet,
the child and the clown,
the idiot and the thief.

All these, and more you kiss,
when you kiss me.

a sorry crown

Dyed, dead, permed hair,
pasted on balding pates,
makes a sorry crown
on waxwork heads.

Death outside is denied
to death inside,
and the night life
of puppets on strings
goes on.

reds and blacks

Once I shone upon the world
a black sun,
and all was sealed
from alien eyes,
but a red nightmare awoke the night
of the black sun
and squirming black held the writhing red
in trembling arms.

And thus it is
that reds and blacks have come to be
the shades of my soul.

Yes, I'm a devotee
of dark deities,
a keeper of gory altars,
and if you'll come.
I'll take you round this world
of reds and blacks.

Look!
There's the radiant red
of the rose on the bough,
and there, look at the wounded red
of the rose on the grave.
Come, touch,
there's the ebon black
of black breasts,
and here,
the black of the bruises
of a battered baby.

Here!
Look at the martyr's face,
once red with pious blood,
and now a putrid black.

And there, on the horizon,
you can see the black
that has blackened the heavens,
being chased away by the red
that is tearing through dawn
to let the day in.

a bad collage

I tear tissue with the lancet,
treat it with acid and alkali,
and smear it
on slide, after slide, after slide....

And I do that
with an unerring sense of purpose,
and with the same
unerring sense of purpose,
my hands lift the cup of poison
to my lips,
my legs run to the cliff
to hurl me into the sea,
my eyes go dim,
my ears deaf.

It is a house
divided against itself,
a story without a thread,
a bad collage.

the darlings
of deity

Lovely as lotus-blooms,
from a centre they arched away.
The darlings leaned back their heads
in slow motion.
Meanwhile through a trick
of the sick-with-life tissue,
their brows grew grave
like the brows of corpses.

And soon,
the cancerous splitting of cells
and the self-slaughter rampant in life
triggered off the return
of chaos.

Then the dying echo
of a Parthian shot[6] was heard,
as death, the deathless antagonist,
awoke in one,
and then in another, and another, and another
of the grave-grey swarms
of the darlings
of deity.

he knows
for he lives off death

Have you questions
about life and death?
Take them to the vulture.
He knows,
for he lives off death.

A tiger pounces on a bull,
as it stands unaware,
beside a withered tree.

A vulture,
perching on the only limb
of the withered three,
waits –
aware and serene –
looking down at life and death
play their ancient game.

Mauled and mangled,
the bull soon dies.
The vulture descends,
and settles down
to a hearty meal.

Take your questions
to the vulture.
He knows.

the wail

The wail arose from the depths
of the pit of nothingness,
where life lay dying.

'Lift me', it begged,
'lift me out of this pit
of nothingness.
Put me back among my illusions
of reality and truth,
of meaning and form,
of value and purpose,
for that is where I belong'.

I heard,
and drew closer to see
who it was that wailed thus.
I shuddered.
It was everyone,
everywhere,
always.

· Section E ·
The Auriga

the good news is
they're breeding apace

In the beginning was the slime,
and in the depths of the slime
was the seed that sprouted
into living death and dying life –
the constant couple.

Aeons later,
to seek out more room
to fill with their kind,
the couple built a flying cave,
and in it left for outer space
to colonise the stars.
And the good news is
that there, among stars,
they're breeding apace.

a special god
of a special people

A special god
of a special people
commanded his host of angels thus:
'Let my chosen ones be given
the best of everything.
Let them have their fill
at the spring of life.'

The special god
of the special people went on:
'Let my chosen ones be
the undisputed monarchs
of their harems.
See to it that they live
for ever smothered
with breasts and bellies.

And, much pleased with himself,
the special god
of the special people
left the scene.

the will
of our lord

For a last earthly gift to himself
a pharaoh wanted a pyramid,
taller than the tallest.

His builders built and built
until they had to stop
for want of stone.
But the pyramid wasn't yet taller
than the tallest.
Most resourcefully, therefore,
the desperate builders resorted
to wrecking an existing pyramid
for its stones.
When challenged,
the builders explained,
'We are only fulfilling the will
of our lord.'

in dusk,
at eventide

Having said the last word
on the fate of the world,
when the prophet walked back
from the seat of the gods,
in dusk, at eventide,
a contemptible piece of rope,
that lay in his path,
triggered him back to his beginnings.
'Snake!', hissed the very seed of man in him.
Only moments ago, fearless and firm,
he had uttered the word that had within it
the beginning, the middle and the end
of everything he knew,
and everything he didn't,
and now he stood
frozen with terror.

He stood frozen with terror,
until his feet, knowing better,
led him back to the doorstep,
where mate and child waited,
in dusk
at eventide.

in the blackmarble hall

In the blackmarble hall
of a hundred columns
they were holding the ceremony of riddance
in the presence of the winged bull,
the divine beetle,
and the royal cobra,
while the captive hero wrestled
with the king's wrestler,
and the doomed demon lovers in chains
looked on.

Soon, the show came to an end,
as all shows do,
and had to make way
for another.

'Next', the supreme illusionist shouted.

And from the eastern gate
of the blackmarble hall
of a hundred columns,
emerged a prophet's mantle and hood,
and a torchlight procession
of the faithful,
with many a sarcophagus held on shoulders,
in dumb show followed,
and the high priest,
with half-shut feline eyes,
watched the torchlight procession
meander from the earth-world
to worlds beyond,
and pleased with his game,
smiled.

**a dream
within a dream**

Tell me, spacemen,
when you swung into space,
did its crescent arms
rock you to comfort?
Or did you find yourself
face to face
with a scimitar-wielding foe,
wanting to gore you to death?

Or was it all a dream
within a dream?

sleepwalking hordes
of the feeble–minded

Beware of dogma.
Dogma cripples reason
with temptation,
beheads it with terror,
and carries the carcass aloft
as the trophy of its triumph,
forever herding sleepwalking hordes
of the feeble-minded
to the ever-hungry pit
of mindlessness.

make–believe
of make–believe

At the launch site
some players staged a make-believe
of a make-believe,
showing apes aping men,
and men looking on,
in alien disgust.

And while men looked on,
the homesick apes,
riding mutant freaks,
travelled all the way,
from the launching site
to the forest of their forefathers,
and back –
only to find the audience
gone.

· Section F ·
The Ara

the promised one

In search of the promised one,
the devil swam across rivers,
wandered from wilderness to wilderness,
climbed to the top of the tallest tree,
and looked, and looked,
and, at long last, espying the promised one,
he shouted in joy,
'There he is, I see him!
There, in the distant black hole
among the trees!
A flitting shadow, a shadowy shape,
alive, astir, gibbering!
Aha, I've found him, he is mine.'
And, at his command,
his mighty horde marched forth in triumph
towards the promised one.

Hanging in hairy nude,
upside down from the branch of a tree,
the monkey gazed in dismay
at the marvelling, gloating horde
that approached apace,
until his yogic vision revealed unto him
things with their right side up.
"Oh, they're coming for me,
their promised one,"
he gibbered in horror, and wondered
where to turn to escape their clutches.

But, alas,
nothing could save him now.
They caught him,
and tied his hands together,
and together they tied his feet,
and carried him along,
hung from a springy shaft on their shoulders.
They took him to many a zoo,
and animal show,
until the keeper of the mortuary got him,
and shoved him
down the mouth of the incinerator,
wherein, in a moment,
he was ashes.

at the end
of the rope

At the end of the rope
a monkey danced –
a starving, naked,
squeaking, squealing wretch.
Away from the forests
of his ancestors,
he danced to a crowd of kith and kin,
all at the ends of their own ropes,
screaming with joy,
while hidden in the crowd.
I winced in twofold shame –
the shame of the monkey that danced,
and the shame of the one
who held the other end
of the rope.

**shelter –
any shelter**

In our fishbowl
I found a fish cosily lodged
in the skeleton of another.
'Damned cannibal,
brainless beast,
soulless ghoul', I hissed,
outraged, aghast!

Or was it just another bit of life,
that had managed to find shelter –
any shelter?

worm's lament
(a monologue)

'Oh man, did you have to come
to this world,
this valley of worms, this, my home?

'Mighty monster!
You wrecked our homes,
why, then, did you spare
this wormy, slimy life of mine?
I say, why did you let your foot
swerve away to leave me alive?

'It's not that I see any good in you, man,
but, tell me,
O dispenser of life and death to worms,
why did your foot swerve,
leaving me unhurt,
to crawl for ever
under the Himalayan weight of life?

'O god of gods, did you hope
to prove to yourself thus
the quality of your spirit?
What if I were my brother,
the magnificent serpent –
the one that performed better
than you and your god?
 Would that have made a difference?

'But now, doomed to live.
I know not what to do.
Tell me if you would have me vanish
into the rare comfort of my blind burrow.
Or, shall I, like a good, little gadget,
go on tilling your earth, O king?

'Man, are you really the size you look,
or is it my worm's eye-view
that makes you loom colossal?

'And where is your curiosity, man?
Didn't you wish to see
what your foot could do to a worm –
How it could crush it
to a smudge of slime?

'How I wish I knew, man,
what turned your foot away.
Could it be the urge
to extend my misery
by letting my loathsome life
last a little longer?
Or, did the anatomy of your foot
know the meaning of the death of a worm?
Did it shrink away
from the terror of the event?

* * *

'Oh, what's the point
of questioning the brute!
Let me revel
in my triumphant thrust
through this yet infertile layer of earth.
I've pierced it now –
yes....but........
what if that particular human foot
hadn't swerved?
What if another foot,
not given to easy swerves,
had crushed me?'

the other side
of the picture

My young head bent down,
my eyes glued
to the picture on my knees,
excited, intrigued, maddened with the urge
to discover the other side
of the picture.
I felt it with fingertips, smelt it,
turned it round and round
and turned it over again and again,
but nothing availed.

And even now that I'm older,
and should know better.
I cannot shut my eyes,
even if my winkless gaze blinds me.
I cannot, I cannot keep from looking
for the other side
of the picture.

the laggard bidder

The laggard bidder slept
at the back of the auctioneer's,
as he always did.

He slept,
until the doors opened.
The auction had begun again.
He moved towards the front
to make his usual 'better-than-before' bid,
but his wits,
befogged, befuddled,
held him half way up with the question.
'Why, why indeed?'
and a shade more lost than before,
back to his corner he went,
and slept,
until the doors opened again.

· Section G ·
The Pegasus

of hungry cats
and immortal pigeons

You are doomed.
Your back is against the boundary
of the universe,
and in front
is the past-to-future
arrow of time[7].
You want to escape to freedom.
What can you do?

It's easy.
All you have to do
is to close your eyes,
and with the help of imaginary numbers[8],
move into imaginary time[9],
and before you know,
the boundary will go,
and you will be free
to escape to freedom.

Free like the imaginative pigeon,
who, when he saw the cat approaching,
closed his eyes
to the world of hungry cats,
and moved into the world
of immortal pigeons.

the anthropic principle[10]

In the matter of self-promotion
we haven't been very discreet.

They say it was Protagoras [11]
who had the impudence to declare
that man was the measure
of all things.

Now, how big is the step
from that delusion
to the anthropic principle –
the philosophical rattle
that science has recast and repainted
to make a noise with?

quantum,[12] string,[13] twistor[14]

Take a dimensionless point,
if you can find one.
Give it dimension,
and you have your quantum.

Stretch the point,
and you have your string.
Twist it,
and you have your twistor.

Now, with your quanta [15],
strings,
and twistors,
you can fill all emptiness
of mind
and of matter.

**a sacrificial offering
of antiparticles**[16]

Driven by a compulsive urge
to know what wouldn't be known,
and to do what wouldn't be done
an astrophysicist travelled
to the event horizon [17] of a black hole [18]
and set up lab.

Now, though he was committed
to knowing what wouldn't be known
and doing what wouldn't be done,
he didn't have the heart
to interfere
with the real universe.
So he did the next best thing.

Instead of the real universe
he used its mirror image
and in place of particles [19]
he used antiparticles
but dared not touch
the course of time.
And he waited.

All went well.

Emboldened, he made his final move.
He reversed the course of time too,
upon which the universe
broke away from the hold
of the laws of physics.

All seemed lost.

However, before the unchained giant
got quite out of hand,
our resourceful astrophysicist
quickly made a sacrificial offering
of antiparticles
to the ever hungry black hole
who readily swallowed the lot
and, to return the favour,
hitched back the universe
to the laws of physics.

All went well, again.

(And let this happier sequel
to the story
be put on record too,
that our astrophysicist achieved
instant fame
as the redeemer
of the laws of physics
of his universe.)

the wayfarers
of the elsewhere[20]

It seems
superstrings[21] or no superstrings,
a 'grand unified theory'[22]
without gravity,
will not do,
nor will relativity
without quanta,
despite the best that the wizards
of the subatomic wonderland
could do.

What *will* do then?

Or is it,
that for us,
the wayfarers
of the elsewhere,
nothing will ever do?

· Section H ·
The Serpens

Sheshnag[23]
in the basket of ribs

Agni[24], come,
come in peace,
closer, closer, closer come.
Take me, feast on me.
I am your own.
Om[25] .....shanti[26] .....shanti.....shanti.

Agni, I am corrupt earth.
Cleanse me, god.
Burn me to my purest self,
so that I can hear the rumble
of arriving.....arriving.....arriving
of Sheshnag,
the world-immense lord,
reclining on his star-spangled couch,
approaching apace,
from beyond the universe,
his imperial head arched
to the highest of heavens,
his endless shape bridging the void
between the world of Brahma[27]
and the kingdom of Yama[28],
till, in the farthest reaches
of eternal night,
the monarch is home,
in the basket of my ribs.
Om.....shanti.....shanti.....shanti.....

the sunbright soul

Go, my heart,
climb the mighty arch
of the ever wakeful cobra's neck,
crowned with a head
carved out of benumbing terror,
bejewelled with bedevilling eyes
that no veil, no darkness know.

Go, my heart,
and with the head of the cobra
merge!

And when the cobra's head,
and you, my heart, are one,
the glistening black glory
of the cobra's sunbright soul
will be mine too!

in Banaras[29]

The tentacles of my memory
are recoiling
along the existence-extinction continuum.

I remember the days and nights
of my life in death,
asleep in corpses,
in the quiet of graves.

I wish I could return
to my life in death,
and the wanton pleasure
of that symbiotic cohabitation.

Ah, that was the time
when life and death
danced and danced and danced,
like the anklet-laden feet
of a temple dancer dancing to Shiva[30],
her gazelle eyes wondering and worshipping
and the curves of her redolent presence
melting in music,
in a temple in Banaras.

Such are the tics
our protoplasmic clay is corrupt with,
and will, for ever, be slave to an infinity
of dislodged, disowned, desolate ghosts.

the wondering,
wide–eyed lotus[31]

The prince, sitting on a rush mat,
shed no shadow,
and let his inner light
gild the temples of heaven.

But, as the princess emerged
from the depths
of the wine-dark sea of fulfilment,
the prince's grip on emptiness loosened,
and he rose to his feet,
ran to her,
and held her in fond arms,
and the honey of their lips flowed
into the wanting void of their souls,
while the sandalwood trees around
spread their fragrance far and wide,
and the wide-eyed lotus,
in the pond nearby
wondered as never before.

**song
of never know**

'I know'
is the burden of the song
of never know,
that fills
the shell of the world.

Round and round the singers go,
around the centre of never know,
while the grove is all gold,
with basant[32] and its maids,
who sing the truth
of bhakti[33] and love,
which they seem to know
rather well.

And the song of never know,
that fills the shell of the world,
keeps pouring unbidden
into listening ears,
until knowing,
and not knowing,
and seeming to know, are the same,
and the grove, all gold,
with basant and its maids,
is everywhere.

Jinni[34]

Yet again,
the greatest teller of tales began:
'Of all the makers and tellers of tales
I'm the greatest, the best.
I'll tell you my masterpiece –
a tale that is truer than truth itself.

'Listen,' he said,
'in the beginning I was small.
Ah, how small, you will never know.
Then, while I grew bigger and stronger
everything other than me
shrank and weakened.
Power-mad, I decided to give
a shape and a name to my power.
I willed with all my might,
and my womb delivered Jinni,
the mightiest of monsters.
With loving care,
I taught my flesh and blood, this Jinni,
all the tricks of the game of power –
to coo, to hiss,
to growl, to howl,
the winsome smile, the fearsome frown,
and now and then, in play,
I let him raze to the ground,
with donkey kicks,
worlds bigger and better
than all the heavens.'

'But, then,' he went on,
'for reasons yet unknown,
Jinni began to decay from within,
until all that was left of him
was the feeble glow
of a dying fire,
and a woeful voice
that came from the fire, said,
'Save me, my source and sustenance.
In you alone I can exist,
for you alone are the void,
vacuous enough to hold me'.

And ending his tragic tale,
the greatest teller of tales wailed:
'I heard, and cried out,
'No, no! Death dare not touch you.
You are mine.
You are me'.
But it was too late,
Jinni was dead,
finally dead,
dead for ever'.

· Section I ·
The Cygnus

Mrs. H.

The subject was fantasies.
'For example', she said to us,
a class of eleven post-graduates,
'while driving up here this morning,
I thought I had eleven breasts,
with eleven infants
sucking lustily at them'.

It was the end of the term,
when, with puzzling abruptness,
she started wearing jewellery,
most noticeable of which
were her gold earrings –
the gold earrings which reminded me
of my dream.

'I dreamt of you', I said,
as she finished her last lecture on Freud.
'You were a corpse that wore
those gold earrings of yours,
and you smiled invitingly.'
She smiled,
and lit another cigarette,
at which she sucked lustily.
'Mother-fixation, frustration, aggression',
she said at last,
dreamily gazing at me,
and my dream corpse.

my pet
who died 'naturally'

'You know I can look after pets',
I said to my father,
'and this time I want
an unusual pet', I declared.
'Not just any pet.
An unusual pet is what I want',
I insisted.
'Will you get me one, Dad?
Promise?', I anxiously asked.

'Yes', said my father.

True to his promise,
my father got me
a baby alligator
for a pet.
Most lovingly I put my precious pet
in a pool I had dug all day.†
But the pool turned out
to be too small for him,
and soon he died.

'Our baby alligator has died, Dad',
I told my father,
hoping for his sympathy
in my hour of sorrow.

'Naturally', said my father.

'Naturally!' – what could it mean?
I wondered then,
as I wonder now.

† in a warm climate somewhere

what a glorious red marvel[†]

The sun had to shine
for days on end, before this,
the prettiest of our tulips opened.
And what a glowing red marvel it was!

We rejoiced.

But soon we noticed
it was closing,
and we couldn't do a thing
to stop it.
What had we done
to be punished so?

The sun returned again and again,
shining brighter and brighter,
longer and longer,
coaxing our tulip to open.

It did not.

Closed it stands there,
with its large velvet petals,
firmly collected in grim defiance,
while many a tulip around it,
wide open in odious abandon,
is getting all the sun it can soak.

Will anything win it back
into our world?
What must we do?

[†] While writing the last stanza of this poem I suddenly realised that the poem was not only about the tulip but also about a very pretty six–year old daughter of a dear friend. Most sadly, something similar has happened to the lovely little girl. I hope and pray that a miracle happens and she returns to normality.

beautiful eyes

Despite what the priest and the judge
have to say to damn him,
the eyes of the young thief
are beautiful,
and to the one who would listen
they say,
'Not only is the priest's sermon pointless,
it's deceitful too.
Not only is the judge's verdict groundless,
it's vindictive too.'

room for growth

'Room for growth,
room for growth,
room for growth', he kept saying.
It made me sick.
'There's room for growth
in everything, everywhere, all the time',
he said again.
'In death too?', I asked,
hoping to annihilate him
with the impact of my supreme wisdom.

Ignoring my interruption,
as one would the expected little bark
of a pup,
he went on:
'Yes, like a foetus,
everything must grow to fill
that ever present room for growth.'

The pathetic claptrap went on and on.

Fed up beyond all endurance,
I got up
and strode out of the lecture theatre,
angry, resentful, anxious.
Back in my cubicle
I just sat,
foetus small, foetus feeble, foetus blind,
not knowing what to do
with my infinite room for growth.

mirror
of your soul

You can see your soul
mirrored in your love.
What kind of love is yours?
Is it the bowl of a beggar?
If it is, that's what your soul is –
the bowl of a beggar.
Or, is it the gift
of a generous heart?
If it is, that's what your soul is –
the gift of a generous heart,
to you,
and to the one you love.

bliss

Often, after a long, hard day,
when I switch off the light,
and curl up in bed,
the whole of me relaxing wholly,
a strange kind of happiness
comes over me –
a kind of chaste ecstasy,
sweet with the honey of 'having arrived',
ripe with the richness
of the ultimate reward.

For some
death must be a similar experience,
only unfathomably more blissful.

· Section J ·
The Apus

in a Sylhet[35] tea garden

They are singing and dancing
of marriage and of birth,
of breeze and of bower,
of rain and of rice,
of the bride who bore a score of sons
and a couple of daughters,
the daughters who were married
to the princes who came
from the hills in the north.

They sing and they dance,
and they giggle in glee,
and nudge each other
as they gather tea leaves
in the baskets on their backs.

Here, look at this one –
her basket will be full very soon,
and her dancing and singing,
and giggling with glee,
and bending and unbending,
and sideways swinging will end,
and the glow on her face
will vanish as she enters her hut –
the hovel where the demon
of total despair
and untold anguish
waits for her
in the dark.

masculine prowess

An arm slashes a throat.
A jet of warm blood
hits the killer's face.
The slashed throat gurgles
for a while.
The victim dies.

The job done,
the killer leaves the scene,
proud of his masculine prowess.

the saving grace
of humanity

Discord, destruction, death
are natural to nature.
One of the forms,
nature gave to them,
was man.
However, he, unhappy soul,
turned out to be more of an evil
than nature could handle,
and would have gladly
got rid of him.

Nevertheless,
finding the creature
rather interesting,
nature decided to keep him.
But first, his evil
had to be counterbalanced
by good.
And that was the holy purpose,
for which nature created woman –
the saving grace
of humanity.

homo insipiens

Man is not all human,
for he is also the brute
that is hidden within him.

Woman is all woman,
that is, all human.
There is no brute lurking in her.

To man,
life is a tree to cut down,
an animal to slaughter,
a throat to strangle,
a heart to stab,
and generally,
his instinct is to be
as big a curse on earth
as possible.

To woman,
life is the foetus she carries,
the infant she feeds,
the child she rears,
the youth she tames,
and the aged she nurses,
and generally,
her instinct is to be
the ultimate blessing
for humanity.

And the irony is,
that, on woman,
the most deserving of her creatures,
the true homo sapiens,
nature has thrust, as mate,
man, the least deserving living thing,
best described
as homo insipiens.

Abbreviations used in the notes

1. B.H.T. *A Brief History of Time from the Big Bang to Black Holes,* 1989 reprint. Author: Stephen W. Hawking.

2. C.E. *Collier's Encyclopedia.*

3. D.H.M.D. *Classic Dictionary of Hindu Mythology and Religion, Geography, History & Literature* by John Dowson.

4. D.H.S. *A Dictionary of Hinduism* Publisher: Routledge & Kegan Paul, Authors: Margaret & James Stutely.

5. E.B. *Encyclopaedia Britannica,* Inc. 1973 edition.

6. E.B.M. *The Encyclopaedia Britannica, (Macropaedia),* 1985 edition.

7. E.R.M.E. *The Encyclopaedia of Religion,* 1987 edition, Editor–in–Chief: Mircea & Elliade

8. N.A.U. *The New Ambidextrous Universe,* 1990 edition, Author: Martin Gardner.

9. S.S.T.E. *Superstrings and the search for the Theory of Everything.* 1988, Author: E. David Peat.

Notes on the Titles of the Sections

A. The Monoceros:
The Unicorn. A constellation of the Southern Hemisphere.

B. The Phoenix:
A legendary Arabian bird said to set fire to itself and rise from the
ashes every five hundred years. A constellation of the Southern
Hemisphere.

C. The Chameleon:
A constellation of the Southern Hemisphere.

D. The Lupus:
The Wolf. A constellation of the Southern Hemisphere.

E. The Auriga:
The Charioteer. A constellation of the Northern Hemisphere.

F. The Ara:
The Altar. A constellation of the Southern Hemisphere.

G. The Pegasus:
The Winged Horse. A constellation of the Northern Hemisphere.

H. The Serpens:
The Serpent. A constellation of the Northern Hemisphere.

I. The Cygnus:
The Swan. A constellation of the Northern Hemisphere.

J. The Apus:
The Bird of Paradise. A constellation of the Southern Hemisphere.

Notes on expressions in the text
marked with a number

1. **red shift:** The shift in the spectral lines of starlight towards the red end of the spectrum when the star is travelling away from us.
2. **homotransplant:** a transplant obtained from a member of the same species
3. **heterotransplant:** a transplant obtained from a member of a different species
4. **autotransplant:** a transplant obtained from the body of the recipient
5. **Hades:** in Greek mythology, the nether world abode of the souls of the dead.
6. **Parthian shot:** a shot like a Parthian archer shooting at the enemy while feigning flight
7. **arrow of time:** 'The increase of disorder or entropy with time is one example of what is called an arrow of time, something that distinguishes the past from the future, giving a direction to time. B.H.T. -- Hawking
8. **imaginary numbers:** 'There are....special numbers (called imaginary) that give negative numbers when multiplied by themselves.' B.H.T. -- Hawking
9. **imaginary time:** 'Time measured using imaginary numbers.' B.H.T. -- Hawking
10. **anthropic principle:** We see the universe the way it is because if it were different, we would not be here to observe it. – B.H.T. -- Hawking
11. **Protagoras** (c. 490-after 421 B.C.) the first and the most famous of the Greek Sophists. His work entitled 'Truth' began with the statement 'Man is the measure of all things.....' – E.B.
12. **quantum:** The quantum is the indivisible unit in which waves may be emitted or absorbed. – B.H.T. -- Hawking
13. **string:** elementary particle, considered as a vibrating, rotating string, not a point particle – S.S.T.E. -- Peat

14. **twistor:** Twistors are mathematical structures that define the motions and spins of massless particles. – N.A.U. -- Gardner

15. **quanta:** see 'quantum'

16. **antiparticles:** An antiparticle is a subatomic particle.... having the same mass, average lifetime, etc., as the particle (see) to which it corresponds, but having the opposite sign of electric charge, etc.

17. **event horizon:** the boundary of a black hole – B.H.T. -- Hawking

18. **black hole:** a region of space-time from which nothing, not even light, can escape, because gravity is so strong – B.H.T. -- Hawking

19. **particles:** A particle is a body whose spatial extent and internal motion and structure, if any, are negligible.

20. **elsewhere, the:** The elsewhere is the region of space-time that does not lie in the future or past light cones of an event. (event: a point in space-time specified by its time and place. Light-cone: a surface in space-time that marks out the possible directions from light rays passing through a given event) – B.H.T. -- Hawking

21. **superstrings:** Superstrings are solitons trapped in the vacuum state of the universe. (A soliton.... is a solitary wave that, for one reason or another, keeps its size and shape permanently, or at least for a long time.) – N.A.U. -- Gardiner

22. **grand unified theory:** A theory that unifies the electromagnetic, strong and weak forces. (Electromagnetic force: The force that arises between particles with electric charge, the second strongest of the four fundamental forces. (Strong force: the strongest of the four fundamental forces with the shortest range of all. Weak force: the second weakest of the four fundamental forces, with a very short range). – B.H.T.-- Hawking

23. **Sheshnag. same as Sesa:** 'Remainder.' The residue of the world, shaped out of the cosmic waters of the abyss. The thousand-headed cosmic serpent (naga), also called Ananta, the 'Endless or Infinite One'. The head of Sesa sustains the earth:.....As a theriomorphic (depicted in the form of a beast) form of Visnu. Sesa is a kind of demiurge (the term used by Plato in the 'Timaeus' to designate the intermediary maker of the world, whose ashes sink into the primordial waters (representing the undifferentiated state of the cosmos), leaving only Visnu and Sesa to continue the work

of creation. Visnu reclines on the coiled form of Sesa, the coils symbolising the endless revolutions of Time. – D.H.S.

24. **Agni:** Agni is the god of fire in ancient and traditional India. Derived from an Indo-European root, the Sanskrit word agni (fire) is related to such other forms as Latin 'Ignis' in the Lithuanian 'ugnis'. A cognate appears in Hittite text .... in the name 'Ak gnis'. Although his mythological and ritual roots are reflected in Old Irish, Roman and Iranian sources, the peculiar development of the god of fire as Agni owes as much to the ritualizing tendencies, the priestly vision, and the strong asceticism of the Indian context as it does to the god's Indo-European heritage. – E.R.M.E.

25. **Om:** a contraction of the sounds /a/, /u/, and /m/, the most sacred of the Sanskrit syllables....the articulated syllable par excellence, the eternally creative divine word.....Om is a particle of pious salutation.... The sacred syllable is divided into its four phonetic components, representing the four states of the mind, or consciousness: /a/ is related to the awakened state, /u/ to the dream state, /m/ to the dreamnless sleep, and the syllable as a whole to the fourth state, 'turiya', which is beyond words and is itself the One, the Ultimate, the Brahman..... – E.R.M.E.

26. **shanti:** equanimity, tranquillity

27. **Brahama:** The first member of the Hindu triad (the other two of which are Visnu and Siva): the supreme spirit manifested as the active creator of the universe. He sprang from the mundane egg deposited by the supreme cause. – D.H.M.D.

28. **Yama:** The ruler and judge of the dead. He is called the 'Restrainer', from 'yam', 'to curb', etc., and hence 'yama', 'cessation', 'end' – D.H.S.

29. **Banaras:** (now 'Varanasi'), on the Ganges, where Siva was known as Vishveshvara (Lord of All), was the centre of his worship. – C.E.

30. **Shiva:** also spelled 'Siva', a primary Hindu deity, figured in the triad (Trimurti) both as the destructive power and the principle of reproduction. – C.E.

31. **lotus:** in Hindi, the flower 'kamal', symbol of the beauty and multiplicity of existence

32. **basant:** the season of the year occurring between winter and summer, spring

33. **Bhakti:** the devotional way of achieving salvation. It demands total submission to the divine.

34. **Jinni:** same as the collective noun 'jinni'; written here with a capital 'J' because of being used as a proper noun. Spiritual beings are classifiable into angels (malaikah), demons (shayateen) and 'jinn' (plural of 'jinni') or genies. The last category includes beings that might be either benevolent or malevolent. The jinn were created out of fire before the creation of Adam, the first man. Capable of both visibility and invisibility, and of assuming various forms, either human or animal, a jinni could be either a help or a hindrance to man. However, by cunning and superior use of intellect, or magic, a man might be able to manipulate a jinni for his own benefit. The jinni are endowed with reason and responsibility but are more prone to evil than man. They, like human beings, have to face eventual salvation or damnation. – Substance taken from E.B.M.

35. **Sylhet:** a district of Bangladesh

ABOUT THE POET

Farman Yusufzai (full name: Farmanullah Khan Yusufzai) was born in undivided India in 1925. He graduated from the University of Lucknow. At partition the family migrated to Pakistan. He took his Master's Degrees in Psychology and English from the University of Lahore. He taught English at colleges in Rawalpindi and Karachi and was an active member of the Pakistan Writers' Guild. He came to London in 1965 and for a while worked for a research degree in English Literature at the Birkbeck College, University of London, while teaching at a High School. He obtained the Diploma in Educational Guidance from the University of Reading in 1972. In 1987 his services were transferred to a language project.

Farman Yusufzai retired two years ago and has since been teaching English as a part-time lecturer at a local college.

Besides English poetry, Farman Yusufzai also writes poetry in Urdu. A collection of his Urdu ghazals was published in 1987. So far as we know he is the only poet, past or present, who has published original poetry in both English and Urdu (not translations) in book form.

At present Farman Yusufzai is working on two collections of his aphorisms, one in English and the other in Urdu. After the publication of these works he intends to devote more time to his literary and philosophical group, the 'All-Inclusive Understanding Circle'.

Woodfield Publishers, 1992

99